holiday *Hearts*

holiday *Hearts*

recipes by

PAMELA SHELDON JOHNS

crafts by

JENNIFER BARRY DESIGN

photography by

SCOTT PETERSON

TEN SPEED PRESS

BERKELEY · TORONTO

A Kirsty Melville Book

Ten Speed Press
Box 7123
Berkeley, California 94707
www.tenspeed.com

Distributed in Australia by Simon & Schuster Australia, in Canada by Ten Speed Press Canada,
in New Zealand by Southern Publishers Group, in South Africa by Real Books, in Southeast Asia by Berkeley Books,
and in the United Kingdom and Europe by Airlift Book Company.

Concept and Design: Jennifer Barry Design, Sausalito, California
Photography: Scott Peterson, San Francisco, California
Layout Production: Kristen Wurz
Copy Editor: Barbara King
Food Stylist: Pouké Halpern
Prop Stylist: Carol Hacker / Tableprop, San Francisco
Editorial Assistance: Blake Hallanan

Library of Congress Cataloging-in-Publication Data
Johns, Pamela Sheldon, 1953–
Holiday hearts : a collection of inspired recipes, gifts,
and decorations / recipes by Pamela Sheldon Johns ; crafts by Jennifer Barry ;
photography by Scott Peterson.
p.   cm.
Includes index.
ISBN 1-58008-420-6
1. Valentine's Day cookery.   2. Valentine decorations.
I. Barry, Jennifer.   II. Title.
TX739.2.V34 J65   2002
641.5'68--dc21   2002006410

Printed in China

10 9 8 7 6 5 4 3 2 1 — 06 05 04 03 02

Acknowledgments

Pamela Sheldon Johns wishes to thank her two best sweethearts, Alaia and Courtney,
for their love and support (and willingness to taste everything!).
A big thank you to Philippa Farrar for her expert help with recipe testing, to Barbara King
for her meticulous copyediting, and to the world's best collaborator, Jennifer Barry.

Jennifer Barry would like to thank the following individuals for their help on
this book project: Ten Speed publisher Kirsty Melville, for her enthusiastic support of the book;
Ten Speed editor Holly Taines White and production manager Hal Hershey, for shepherding
the book to its beautiful finished state; my coauthor Pamela Sheldon Johns, who always makes
working on a book together a labor of love; photographer Scott Peterson, food stylist Pouké Halpern,
and prop stylist Carol Hacker of Tableprop, for making the photography so beautiful and
for being so much fun to work with that it never seems like work; my book design
and office colleague Kristen Wurz, for being the best there is at everything she does;
Leslie Anne Barry, for her early help with the design of this new book in our *Holiday* series;
Muriel Schmalberg Ullman, for her beautiful hand-painted artwork used as
a background for the sachets; Aidan Johnson for sharing his time and showing us the art
of eating a Popsicle; and Blake Hallanan for her continuous editorial support.

Introduction

Historical Hearts

"I love you with all my heart," whispers my five-year-old daughter, two tiny hands clasped together on her chest. She has handed me a drawing, hearts of every color surrounding a large red heart with a smiling face. And it's not even Valentine's Day!

Throughout time, the heart has been a symbol of human emotion. We speak of a wounded heart, a heart broken or stolen; we suffer heartache; and our hearts fill with joy. We learn poetry by heart, respond in a heartbeat, and attempt to get to the heart of most matters. Western civilization can trace the origins of Valentine's Day to an ancient Roman fertility festival called Lupercalia, dedicated to Faunus, the Roman god of agriculture, as well as honoring Juno, the goddess of marriage; Romulus and Remus, the founders of Rome; and Lupercus, the god who kept the citizens safe from wolves. On February 14, the eve of the celebration, it was the custom to choose a lover for the year by drawing names on slips of paper from a jar.

When this pagan festival evolved to a Christian holiday, the church tried to change the image by asking participants to write the names of saints on the slips of paper and to meditate upon that saint's virtues in the next year. The holiday took on a more romantic sentiment when, in 496 C.E., Pope Gelasius declared February 14 the day to honor St. Valentine, patron saint of lovers. Valentine earned sainthood for defying Emperor Claudius II, who ordered that all young men remain single so that they would be strong and dedicated soldiers. Valentine secretly performed marriages for young lovers, and when discovered, was put to death on February 14, 296 C.E. Another legend elaborates that, while in jail, Valentine fell in love with the jailer's daughter and sent her a note signed, "From your Valentine." Some consider this the first valentine.

Some scholars credit Chaucer for inventing the concept of St. Valentine's Day in *Parlement of Foules,* composed around 1380, which takes place "on Seynt Valentynes day,/Whan every soul cometh there to chese [choose] his make [mate]." The oldest known valentine still in existence is a romantic verse written in 1415 by Charles, the Duke of Orleans, to his wife while he was imprisoned in the Tower of London. It is now on display at the British Museum in London. For the most part, however, expressions of love on Valentine's Day were spoken or sung. By the sixteenth century, written valentines began to replace verbal ones. Religious orders created miniature lace-like remembrances with the images of saints or the Sacred Heart, which they sold on Valentine's Day to raise money for charitable works. By the eighteenth century, German cut-paper art and designs were popular in Europe, and this art was eventually imported to England and North America for manufacture.

In Worcester, Massachusetts, in the 1840s, Esther Howland began printing the first commercial valentines in the United States, made from imported lace and fine papers from England. A dynamic entrepreneur at the age of twenty, she also patented the brown shopping bag. In her first year of business she sold $5,000 worth of cards. She created the first assembly line production of cards, employing only women. Not long after, in 1915, Joyce Hall created Hallmark, today the largest producer of greeting cards with a range of thirty languages sold in more than a hundred countries. According to the Greeting Card Association, American consumers purchase more than seven billion greeting cards a year. Valentine's Day cards account for 25 percent, second only to Christmas cards.

With the advent of the Internet, the mode of conveying modern valentine wishes may be changing. Now we can e-mail or video valentines. Even the traditional card business is evolving to include "scratch-and-sniff" cards or cards that record or play auditory messages or music.

Hearts Around the World

A special day for sweethearts is universal. Italy was the birthplace of Saint Valentine. Depending on the source, the story goes that St. Valentine was from Rome or from Terni, a small town in Umbria. And even though it is no longer a church-sanctioned event, Italian lovers still remember and treasure each other on February 14 with romantic meals, love poems, and music.

In France, young girls believe that they will marry the first young man they see on the morning of St. Valentine's Day.

Some historians think that St. Valentine was chosen as the patron saint of lovers because his name sounds like the French word *galantin,* which means lover. Valentine parties have been held in France since the seventeenth century.

England has propagated the sweet notion of February 14 since the 1700s. In the late 1800s, Victorian England probably preferred a written message to the spoken word because such a display of emotion was not fashionable during this period. Often valentines were left anonymously on a doorstep, with elaborate designs that included handmade laces, silk, satin, feathers, flower petals, and gold leaf. Then, as now, it was also a children's holiday with valentine exchanges and heart-shaped treats. Another custom was for children to dress as adults and go caroling for valentine gifts and sweets. In Scotland, sweethearts exchanged ribbons tied into a lover's knot.

In Denmark, children exchange gifts on *Fjortende Februar,* February 14. In Germany, women plant onions on Valentine's Day. Each onion is labeled with the name of a prospective mate. The first onion to sprout will be her love.

Australia has caught onto the trend only in the last ten years, but Australians have taken to it in a big way. In 2001, florists there sold more than four million roses and sweethearts received more than a million boxes of chocolates.

China celebrates *Qi Qiao Jie* on the seventh day of the seventh month in the Chinese lunar calendar (in August of the Western calendar). It originates from a mythical legend of love from ancient times and also observes the Daughter's Festival, a wish for a good marriage.

The Symbols of Love

Sometimes it isn't easy to tell someone how you feel, or maybe you just want to emphasize the words. On Valentine's Day, certain icons have evolved to help us express our feelings. The heart, cupid, flowers, and even birds each send a special message from one heart to another.

Hearts The heart has become the most recognized symbol of Valentine's Day. The Romans believed the heart contained the soul, and to give a heart to another was to share the essence of oneself. The Catholic Church immortalized the image of the Sacred Heart, the physical heart of Jesus, as an object of worship and love, which began to appear in artwork as early as the 1400s. By the 1600s, the heart began to serve as a token of love exchanged between sweethearts. When you think of the ache of longing for another consuming someone, you can easily imagine how the image of cupid's arrow piercing the heart came to be. The heart is central to physical and emotional life.

Cupid In Latin, the word *cupid* means desire. Cupid was the spunky son of Venus, the goddess of love. He carried a bow with a quiver of arrows that could send desire into the hearts of young lovers. According to myth, anyone hit by one of Cupid's arrows would fall deeply in love with the first person he or she saw.

Flowers Since ancient times, flowers have had symbolic importance to many cultures. Even today, many flower-giving traditions are based on the meaning of each flower's sentiment. As symbols of love, flowers reached the zenith of their popularity in nineteenth-century England when a book called *The Language of Flowers* was published equating different varieties with different sentiments of love. Forget-me-nots were said to represent true love; baby's breath symbolized a pure heart; and lilac heralded a first love.

Roses, said to be the favored flower of Venus and Aphrodite, the Roman and Greek goddesses of love, are still the most popular flowers given on Valentine's Day. Over 100 million stems of roses are purchased in the United States for Valentine's Day. White roses stand for true love; red roses are for passionate love; pink roses are for sweethearts; and yellow roses are for friendship. In a bridal bouquet, roses portend happiness. Rosebuds signify youth, purity, and innocence.

Birds People in medieval England and France believed that on Valentine's Day, birds found their mates. Lovebirds symbolize love because they are in the constant company of their mates; you often find them nestled together like sweethearts. Doves also mate for life and are a symbol of loyalty. To dream of a dove is to have a promise of happiness.

Food and Love

One of the most hopeful, and enjoyable, endeavors is our attempt to find love through food. The old adage, "The way to a man's heart is through his stomach," surely also applies to women. The image of lovers feeding each other spoonfuls of caviar by candlelight is a classic Valentine scene. Fantasies abound with regard to whipped cream and strawberries. And chocolate, oh chocolate, in any form causes the most stoic to swoon.

According to the *Encyclopædia Britannica,* an aphrodisiac is a form of stimulation thought to arouse sexual excitement. Such stimulants may include food, alcoholic drinks, and love potions. The article maintains that most of those treatments are based on folklore rather than scientific proof. Still, onions, pine nuts, and fennel have all earned a reputation over the centuries for inspiring love.

Looking for "Love Potion Number Nine"? Try an ancient drink called Hippocras, perhaps created by Hippocrates. Claret (or red Burgundy wine) is blended with ginger, cinnamon, cloves, vanilla, and sugar. Sounds delicious, whatever the other side effects may be.

Science, however, has discovered a foundation for some of our Valentine favorites: wine and chocolate. As you probably know, alcohol in a moderate amount decreases inhibition. (As Shakespeare writes in *Macbeth,* "It provokes the desire, but it takes away the performance," which reminds us that too much spoils the fun.) Most people are pleased to accept a theory regarding the positive effects of chocolate. Consider the abundance of chocolate products that appear on Valentine's Day—everything from sensuous chocolate-dipped cherry truffles to chocolate tattoos to paint on your lover. Chocolate actually contains a chemical substance that causes the body to release endorphins, producing euphoria. No wonder the combination of red wine and chocolate is so wonderful!

Mythology and folk legends have long attributed food products with sexual powers from either their symbolic resemblance to fertility (eggs, nuts, and seeds) or their physical resemblance to erogenous body parts (asparagus, avocados, bananas, carrots, figs, ginseng root, raspberries, and shellfish). In England, women used to eat hard-boiled eggs and put herbs under their pillows to dream of a future lover.

In the end, what could be more sensuous and romantic than a delicious carefully prepared meal shared by two. Cooking together can be romantic as well—the act of sharing, the scents, the beauty, the textures, and the tastes, all prepare us for love.

The Roman poet Seneca had the best advice: "I will show you a love charm without potions, without herbs, without any witch's incantation—if you wish to be loved, love."

In the Holiday Hearts Kitchen

Chocolate How do you define romance? Luscious red ripe strawberries robed in a jacket of dark bittersweet chocolate? Cookies laced with decadent chunks of milk chocolate? No matter how you use it, chocolate is the ultimate Valentine ingredient. Bricks or bars of chocolate are usually of better quality than prepackaged chips. The irregular pieces you get when chopping bricks or bars with a chef's knife add interest to the texture. Choose your preferred chocolate: bittersweet is dark and suggestive, milk chocolate is rich and sensuous, and white chocolate is sweetly romantic.

Pink and Red In the language of love, pink and red are the colors of choice. Pink is associated with innocence and flirtation; red symbolizes the heat of passion. Rather than using artificial colors, we have chosen naturally colored ingredients to bring out our true colors for Valentine's Day.

The best sweets result from intensely colored ingredients such as grenadine, a non-alcoholic syrup that is a sweet reduction of pomegranate juice. Other sweet pink and red foods include rhubarb, apples, blood oranges, guava, raspberries, strawberries, cherries, cranberries, red fruit jams, dried red fruits, red fruit juices, peppermint, and pink and red candies.

Savory pink and red foods include fresh tomatoes, sun-dried tomatoes, pimiento, red bell peppers, beets, red Swiss chard, and red salmon caviar.

Equipment The best time to shop for your Holiday Hearts preparation is February. Stores, catalogs, and Internet sites abound with special muffin pans, cake pans, tart pans, and cookie cutters as well as decorative supplies.

Your basic equipment should include the following: spatulas, pastry brushes, dough scrapers, pastry bags and tips, a wire whisk, dry and liquid measuring cups, and a good set of mixing bowls.

Baking Sheets I prefer to use an aluminum baking sheet lined with parchment paper for cookies. The aluminum heats quickly, and the parchment paper makes for easy cleaning.

Cake Pans and Muffin Tins In addition to a variety of heart-shaped pans, you should have an assortment of round and square cake pans (9-inch diameter is a good standard size). Muffin tins come in three standard sizes and can be used for savory dishes as well as cupcakes and muffins. For the best results in removing cakes and muffins from their pans, be sure to liberally butter the bottom and sides of the pan and dust with flour, tapping to shake out the excess, before filling with the batter.

Cookie Cutters Clearly cookie cutters are essential in the Holiday Hearts kitchen. Simple round cutters with straight or fluted edges are handy for the basics. Hearts come in a vast array of sizes and forms, from traditional symmetrical hearts to more abstract, modernized shapes. Not limited to making cookies, the cutters are useful in shaping savories such as polenta hearts, sweetheart tea sandwiches, and little pizzas with a romantic message. Tiny aspic cutters come in very handy for making miniature cookies and garnishes.

The Way to a Heart

Why wait for February? Any day is a day for romance. It doesn't take much time to make a heart-shaped garnish for a midweek dinner or little treasures to be wrapped and slipped into a pocket or a lunchbox or to serve breakfast in bed.

Many of the recipes in this book can be made ahead or prepped up to the final steps. Planning and preparation are the keys to a romantic encounter. Who wants to spend time running an electric mixer while your sweetheart stands by?

Here are some ideas for making your efforts look great and conveying your message of love:

- Heart-shaped doilies
- Beautiful and unusual containers for presenting baked goods, such as antique candy dishes, glass apothecary jars, or gold or fabric covered boxes lined with parchment or handmade papers
- Edible garnishes such as flowers or heart cutouts
- Flower petals strewn on the table, serving tray, or bed
- Attractive scents: fragrances for the home, scented candles, sachets, flowers, essential oils
- Beautiful wraps, silk ribbons, white laces, boxes, bags, and tissues to present your gift
- Poetry and love messages tucked into cards, presents, or lunchboxes
- Themed music for a romantic meal, such as Tchaikovsky played during a Russian caviar course

baked from the heart

Chocolate Heart Tortes for Two

THIS DECADENT CAKE IS MEANT TO BE SHARED, A PROMISE THAT NO HEARTS WILL BE BROKEN. IT CAN ALSO BE MADE WITH MILK CHOCOLATE FOR A MILDER VERSION, PERHAPS FOR THE FIRST DATE.

5 ounces bittersweet chocolate, coarsely chopped

1/2 cup sugar

6 tablespoons unsalted butter

2 tablespoons Frangelico (hazelnut liqueur)

1/2 cup finely chopped hazelnuts

3 large eggs, separated

Cocoa powder, for dusting

1 cup raspberries, for garnish

Preheat the oven to 300°F. Butter and flour two 5-inch heart-shaped tart pans with removable bottoms.

In the top of a double boiler over medium-high heat, combine the chocolate, sugar, and butter and stir until melted and smooth. Remove from the heat and stir in the Frangelico and hazelnuts. Set aside to cool for 5 minutes. When cooled, whisk in the egg yolks, one at a time. Set aside.

In a clean stainless-steel bowl, whisk the egg whites to stiff peaks. Stir one-third of the beaten whites into the chocolate mixture, then fold in the remaining whites until fully incorporated. Pour the batter into the prepared pans and bake for 30 to 35 minutes, or until a toothpick inserted in the center of the cake comes out clean. Let the cakes cool completely on a rack before removing the sides. Transfer to a serving platter, dust with cocoa powder, and garnish with raspberries. *Serves 2 to 4*

Walnut-Orange Heart Muffins with Candied Orange Zest

ANCIENT ROMANS THREW WALNUTS INSTEAD OF RICE AT WEDDINGS, AS A FERTILITY WISH. HERE THEY ARE PAIRED WITH ORANGES TO MAKE FRAGRANT AND NUTRITIOUS MORNING MUFFINS.

2 oranges

1 cup water

1-3/4 cups sugar

1/2 cup unsalted butter,
at room temperature

2 large eggs

4 tablespoons grated orange zest

1/2 cup sour cream

1 teaspoon baking powder

1/2 teaspoon baking soda

2 cups unbleached all-purpose flour

1/2 cup coarsely chopped walnuts, toasted

Preheat the oven to 375°F. Generously butter a heart-shaped muffin tin.

With a large zester, remove strips of zest from the oranges. Cut the oranges in half crosswise and juice the halves to extract 1/2 cup of juice. Set aside.

In a heavy saucepan, combine the water and 3/4 cup of the sugar, stirring to dissolve. Place over medium heat and bring to a boil. Add the orange zest strips and simmer for 5 minutes. Set aside.

With an electric mixer, beat the remaining 1 cup sugar and the butter together until creamy. Add the eggs one at a time. Add the grated orange zest, sour cream, and the 1/2 cup orange juice.

In another bowl, mix the baking powder and baking soda with the flour and fold gently into the batter. Add 1/4 cup of the toasted walnuts, continuing to fold lightly.

Scoop the batter into the prepared muffin cups. Top each one with a few of the remaining walnuts. Bake for 15 to 20 minutes, or until golden brown and springy to the touch. Turn out onto a rack to cool. Garnish each muffin with 2 or 3 of the candied orange zest strips. *Makes 12 muffins*

Cherry-Lemon Cookie Hearts

A VARIETY OF SHAPES MAKES YOUR COOKIE PLATTER MORE INTERESTING. TRY CUTTING A HEART OUT OF A SQUARE AND SANDWICH IT WITH JAM ON TOP OF ANOTHER SQUARE, THEN BAKE. OR SANDWICH THE LITTLE CUTOUT HEARTS WITH JAM AND BAKE.

1/2 cup (1 stick) unsalted butter, at room temperature

3/4 cup sugar

1 egg

1/2 teaspoon vanilla extract

1 tablespoon heavy cream

2 teaspoons grated lemon zest

1-1/2 cups unbleached all-purpose flour

1/8 teaspoon salt

1/4 teaspoon baking powder

1/2 cup cherry jam

Preheat the oven to 325°F. Lightly butter 2 baking sheets.

In a mixing bowl, cream together the butter and sugar until lightened. Add the egg, vanilla, cream, and lemon zest and mix well.

In another mixing bowl, combine the flour, salt, and baking powder. Add to the first mixture and mix well. Wrap in plastic wrap and refrigerate for 1 hour or overnight.

On a lightly floured work surface, roll out the dough to 1/4 inch thick. Cut into 2-inch squares. Cut out a small heart in the center of half of the squares with a heart-shaped cookie cutter. Place each cut square on top of an uncut square and press the edges together. Prick the top with a fork. Place the cutout hearts on 1 baking sheet and the squares on the other baking sheet. Bake the squares for 10 to 12 minutes and the hearts for 8 to 10 minutes, until golden brown. Cool on a wire rack. When cooled, place a spoonful of jam in the cutout heart of each square. Top with the baked heart. *Makes 2 dozen cookies*

Dried Cranberry Shortbread Cookies

THESE COOKIES ARE BEAUTIFUL AND RUSTIC WHEN CUT INTO HEARTS WITH A VARIETY OF COOKIE CUTTERS.
SPRINKLE WITH CONFECTIONERS' SUGAR WHEN COOL, IF DESIRED.

1 cup (2 sticks) unsalted butter, at room temperature

1/2 cup confectioners' sugar, plus extra for dusting (optional)

1/4 cup coarsely chopped dried cranberries

1/4 cup coarsely chopped walnuts

2 cups unbleached all-purpose flour

Pinch of salt

Preheat the oven to 350°F. Line 2 baking sheets with parchment paper and set aside.

In a mixing bowl, cream the butter until softened, then beat in the confectioners' sugar. Stir in the cranberries, walnuts, flour, and salt and mix well. Press into a large flattened disk, cover well with plastic wrap, and refrigerate for 1 hour.

With a rolling pin, roll out the dough on a floured work surface to a thickness of 1/4 inch. Cut into hearts with cookie cutters. Gather dough scraps into a ball and repeat the process until all of the dough is used. Place on the prepared baking sheets and bake for 20 to 25 minutes, until lightly browned. Let cool completely before dusting with confectioners' sugar. *Makes 2 dozen cookies*

Pink Coconut Custard Hearts with Rose Petals

IN *THE LANGUAGE OF FLOWERS,* PINK ROSEBUDS SIGNIFY TENDER, SWEET LOVE. THIS CUSTARD CAN BE MADE
A DAY AHEAD, COVERED AND CHILLED, AND GARNISHED WITH ROSE PETALS JUST BEFORE SERVING.

1 egg yolk

2 eggs

2 tablespoons grenadine

1/4 cup sugar

Pinch of salt

2 cups milk, scalded

1/4 cup flaked coconut, plus 2 tablespoons for garnish

Fresh untreated pink rose petals, for garnish

Preheat the oven to 325°F. Butter 6 shallow 5-ounce heart-shaped glass ramekins.

In a mixing bowl, beat together the egg yolk, eggs, and grenadine. Add the sugar and salt, beating until the sugar has dissolved. In a slow stream, add the hot milk, beating constantly. Strain through a fine-mesh sieve into a separate bowl. Add the coconut, stir well, and pour into the prepared ramekins.

Place the ramekins in a baking dish and place in the oven. Pour hot water into the baking dish until it reaches the middle of the ramekins' sides. Bake for 45 minutes, or until a knife inserted in the center comes out clean. Allow to cool to room temperature or chill before serving. Garnish with coconut and rose petals.
Serves 6

Heart-Shaped Cinnamon Cake with Brandied Cherries

MOLDED CAKE PANS ARE PERFECT FOR A DENSE COFFEE CAKE SUCH AS THIS. WHEN INVERTED, THE SHAPE HOLDS VERY WELL.

THE BRANDIED CHERRIES ALSO MAKE A NICE VALENTINE GIFT WHEN PACKAGED IN AN ATTRACTIVE JAR TIED WITH A BEAUTIFUL RIBBON.

BRANDIED CHERRIES

1 pound fresh or frozen pitted cherries

2 cups sugar

1 teaspoon cinnamon

3 cups spring water

6 tablespoons good-quality brandy

CINNAMON CAKE

2 tablespoons unsalted butter,
at room temperature

1/2 cup granulated sugar

2 eggs, separated

1/4 cup milk

3/4 cup cake flour

1/4 cup cornstarch

Pinch of salt

2 teaspoons baking powder

1-1/2 teaspoons cinnamon

Confectioners' sugar, for dusting

To make the cherries: In a saucepan, combine the cherries, sugar, cinnamon, and water. Cook over medium heat, stirring frequently, for 5 minutes, until the sugar has dissolved and the cherries have softened. Remove from the heat and stir in the brandy. Place in a clean glass jar and refrigerate overnight or for up to a month.

To make the cake: Preheat the oven to 350°F. Lightly butter a decorative 7-inch heart-shaped cake mold.

In a mixing bowl, beat together the butter and sugar until light and creamy. Add the egg yolks and milk, stirring to mix well. In another bowl, combine the flour, cornstarch, salt, and baking powder. Gently fold into the butter mixture. Do not overmix.

Beat the egg whites until stiff. Fold gently into the batter. Transfer to the prepared cake mold and add the cinnamon, 1/2 teaspoon at a time, swirling into the batter with a fork. Bake for 20 to 25 minutes, until a toothpick inserted in the center comes out clean.

Remove from the oven and allow to cool for 10 minutes. Loosen the sides with a sharp knife and remove from the mold to finish cooling on a wire rack. When cool, dust with confectioners' sugar and serve with the brandied cherries. *Serves 8*

Pistachio-Cherry Biscotti

THESE COOKIES ARE THE PERFECT VALENTINE GIFT FOR A LOVER, RELATIVE, OR FRIEND, AS THEY KEEP
WELL IN AN AIRTIGHT CONTAINER. CHOOSE AN ATTRACTIVE JAR AND TUCK IN A SWEET, HANDWRITTEN SENTIMENT.
DRIED CRANBERRIES ALSO WORK WELL IN PLACE OF THE CHERRIES.

1-3/4 cups cake flour

1-1/4 cups unbleached all-purpose flour

1 teaspoon salt

1 teaspoon baking powder

1/2 teaspoon baking soda

1/2 cup shelled pistachio nuts

1/2 cup dried cherries

4 large eggs

3/4 cup sugar

2 teaspoons vanilla extract

Preheat the oven to 325°F. Line a baking sheet with parchment paper.

In a large bowl, combine the cake flour, all-purpose flour, salt, baking powder, baking soda, pistachios, and cherries. Mix well.

In another bowl, beat the eggs and sugar until creamy. Add the vanilla and mix well. Stir the egg mixture into the dry ingredients, stirring just until blended. Do not overmix.

Transfer the dough to the prepared baking sheet, forming a log about 3 inches wide. Bake for about 30 minutes, until a toothpick inserted into the center comes out clean. Transfer to a wire rack to cool. Decrease the oven temperature to 275°F. Replace the parchment paper on the baking sheet.

Slice the log diagonally into 1/2-inch-wide cookies and place them on the baking sheet. Bake for about 20 minutes, until the cookies are a pale golden brown. Transfer to wire racks to cool.

Makes 2 dozen cookies

Bleeding Heart Brownies

CHOCOLATE AND RASPBERRIES ARE A PERFECT MARRIAGE.

FRESH RASPBERRIES CAN BE USED IN PLACE OF THE FROZEN CUBES FOR A LESS JUICY FILLING.

1 cup frozen raspberries, slightly defrosted

1 cup sugar

4 ounces bittersweet chocolate, coarsely chopped

2 tablespoons unsalted butter

2 tablespoons water

2 eggs

1/2 cup unbleached all-purpose flour

3 ounces bittersweet chocolate, finely chopped

Pinch of salt

Preheat the oven to 325°F. Generously butter 6 cups of a heart-shaped muffin tin.

Place the raspberries and 2 tablespoons of the sugar in a food processor and purée until smooth. Press the raspberry mixture through a fine-mesh sieve to remove the seeds. Divide the raspberry purée among 6 compartments of an ice cube tray and freeze until firm.

In the top of a double boiler over low heat, combine the coarsely chopped chocolate with the butter, water, and remaining sugar. Warm, stirring occasionally, until the chocolate and butter melt. Transfer to a large mixing bowl and set aside to cool for 5 minutes.

When cooled, whisk in the eggs. Add the flour, finely chopped chocolate, and salt, stirring just until moistened. Spoon two-thirds of the mixture into the prepared muffin cups. Press a frozen raspberry purée cube into the batter and cover with the remaining batter.

Bake for 20 minutes, until the sides pull away from the muffin cups and the tops are slightly firm when touched lightly with a finger. Cool for 5 minutes, then invert onto a wire rack until ready to serve. *Makes 6 brownies*

Strawberry-Rhubarb Clafouti

A CLAFOUTI IS A CROSS BETWEEN A PANCAKE AND A PUDDING.

IT IS SOFT AND SENSUOUS AND BEST SERVED WARM.

1-1/4 pounds rhubarb stalks,
leafy ends removed

1 pint strawberries, stemmed

1-1/2 cups sugar

1-1/4 cups unbleached all-purpose flour

Pinch of salt

2 eggs

1-1/4 cups milk

1-1/2 teaspoons vanilla extract

2 tablespoons coarse-grained red sugar, for sprinkling
(available at grocery stores)

Preheat the oven to 425°F. Lightly oil an 8-inch heart-shaped cake pan.

Wash the rhubarb and strawberries in cold water and drain on a kitchen towel. With a paring knife, chop the rhubarb stalks crosswise into 1/2-inch pieces to make 1 quart. Cut the strawberries lengthwise into 1/4-inch slices.

In a mixing bowl, combine 1-1/4 cups of the sugar, 1/4 cup of the flour, and the salt. Add the rhubarb and strawberries and mix well. Transfer to the prepared cake pan. Set aside.

In a bowl, beat the remaining 1/4 cup sugar and the eggs until fluffy; add the milk and vanilla. Add the remaining 1 cup flour and beat well. Pour the batter over the rhubarb mixture and bake for 20 minutes, until the top has set. Sprinkle with the red sugar and bake for another 15 to 20 minutes, until the sugar has melted and the top is golden brown. Allow to cool to lukewarm and serve. *Serves 6*

tabletop hearts

Valentine Placemats

THESE PLACEMATS ARE AN EASY WAY TO PERSONALIZE YOUR OWN VALENTINE TABLE SETTING.
YOU WILL NEED ACCESS TO A PERSONAL COMPUTER, SCANNER, COLOR INK-JET PRINTER,
AND DESKTOP PUBLISHING SOFTWARE, ALL OF WHICH ARE AVAILABLE AT COPY CENTERS NATIONWIDE.

YOU WILL NEED:

Iron

12 by 18-inch cotton or linen placemats

Personal computer and desktop publishing software

Typefaces and copyright-free heart artwork

8-1/2 by 11-inch iron-on transfer paper
for use in ink-jet printers (available at office and
craft supply stores)

Scissors

Masking tape

Bath towel

TO MAKE:

Iron the placemats well before starting project.

Create heart artwork on a personal computer using copyright-free artwork. We used 10 large 2-inch hearts and 4 small 7/8-inch hearts.

Make a template of your placemat design on the computer and size and place the heart artwork to fit comfortably within the template. Print out a copy of your template at full size and set aside. This template will be used later for positioning your iron-on transfers.

Copy and place all the heart artwork in an upright position on a new 8-1/2 by 11-inch page template, leaving a 1/2-inch space between all elements. Choose a color for the hearts. We chose a bright red. Print the hearts on the transfer paper using a color ink-jet printer. Using scissors, cut them out, trimming within 1/8 inch of the printed edge to avoid a glossy halo after ironing.

Tape a placemat to a window or large light box with the placemat template centered underneath it. Using single, small pieces, tape each heart transfer into position.

Remove the placemat from the window or light box and place on top of a clean towel on a hard work surface near an electrical outlet for the iron.

After removing the tape, iron on each transfer according to the ironing instructions that accompany the transfer paper. Let cool for 3 minutes and carefully peel away the transfer backing. Repeat the process for multiple placemats.

Be sure to follow the laundering and ironing instructions that accompany the transfer paper when washing the placemats.

Heart Doily Napkin Rings

DOILIES PROVIDE ENDLESS CREATIVE POSSIBILITIES FOR VALENTINE'S DAY.

SMALL DOILIES WERE USED TO MAKE THESE EASY DOILY AND RIBBON NAPKIN RINGS.

DON'T BE AFRAID TO USE DIFFERENT COLORS AND SIZES OF DOILIES

AND RIBBONS FOR A FESTIVE AND ECLECTIC LOOK FOR YOUR HOLIDAY TABLE.

YOU WILL NEED:

3- or 4-inch paper heart doilies (allow at least
2 per napkin ring)

Ruler

X-acto art knife

14-inch lengths of 1/4- to 1-inch-wide soft ribbon

Napkins

TO MAKE:

Carefully separate the doilies, but leave 2 to 3 doilies attached together for each napkin ring.

Using a ruler and X-acto knife, cut a vertical slit in the middle of each heart 1/8 inch longer than the width of the ribbon you are using.

Thread both ends of a length of ribbon through the slit leaving a large loop on the underside of the heart. Insert a napkin through the loop and pull ribbon ends gently to tighten loop and heart around the napkin, tying the ribbon ends into a bow to secure.

Valentine Flowerpots

CHOOSE YOUR FAVORITE COLORFUL PLANTS AND PRESENT THEM IN SPECIALLY MADE POTS

TO CREATE A FESTIVE CENTERPIECE FOR A VALENTINE PARTY OR HOLIDAY TABLE.

YOU WILL NEED:

Type or script lettering, created on
a personal computer

Ruler

Scissors

Black chalk

Masking tape

3- or 4-inch terra-cotta pots,
one for each word

Pencil

Fine-point permanent marker
(we used a Sanford Sharpie ultra fine point)

Paper towel

TO MAKE:

Select your desired lettering. Size words to fit comfortably on the sides of the pots using a ruler and personal computer or copy machine.

Print out lettering on paper and cut the words into strips, leaving an even 1/2-inch border along the top and bottom. Turn the strips over and cover the backs evenly with black chalk.

Tape each word strip to a pot (with the chalked side against the pot), being careful to align multiple words used on different pots in the same place from the top or bottom edge of the pot. Trace the outlines of the lettering onto the pot with a pencil, being sure to trace along both the inner and outer edges of the letters.

Remove the paper strips and trace over the chalked lettering outlines with a permanent marker and fill in any letter thickness as needed. Wipe off any residual chalk with a paper towel and plant your favorite valentine flower in the pots.

Rose Heart Candle Wreaths

LOVE AND ROSES ARE SYNONYMOUS. THIS EASY CANDLE WREATH MAKES A QUICK HOLIDAY TABLE CENTERPIECE USING A HEART-SHAPED DISH, FLORAL FOAM, AND SWEETHEART ROSES. CHOOSE ROSES OF A SINGLE COLOR OR A MIXTURE OF REDS, PINKS, AND PALE ORANGES FOR A VARIETY OF EFFECTS.

YOU WILL NEED:

Serrated knife

1 block floral foam

7 by 1-inch heart-shaped ceramic dish

3-inch pillar candle

Water

Roses or other firm-stemmed flowers

Sharp knife or floral scissors

TO MAKE:

With a serrated knife, slice the floral foam into 3/4-inch-thick sheets. Place 2 sheets next to each other on a flat surface. Place the heart-shaped dish on top of the foam sheets, centered between the 2 sheets, and trace the dish onto the foam using the tip of the knife. Remove the dish. Place a candle in the center of the heart tracing and trace the circumference of the candle onto the foam with the knife. Remove the candle.

Cut out the heart halves and the center half circles from the foam using the serrated knife and fit the foam into the ceramic dish. Fill halfway with water.

Trim the flower stems to 1 inch from the flower heads with a sharp knife or scissors. Stick the stems into the foam so that none of the foam is showing when all of the flowers are inserted. Place the candle in the center hole.

Keep the foam wet by replenishing water daily. The arrangement will keep for 2 to 3 days at room temperature.

sweet hearts

4

Heart-Shaped Pecan Pancakes with Maple Butter

THESE SWEETHEART PANCAKES ARE MADE WITH EASY-TO-USE RING MOLDS THAT HAVE HANDY UPRIGHT HANDLES. TO SPEED UP THE COOKING PROCESS, YOU CAN USE THREE OR FOUR OF THE MOLDS, WHICH ARE READILY AVAILABLE AT MOST COOKWARE STORES.

MAPLE BUTTER

1/4 cup (1/2 stick) unsalted butter,
at room temperature

3 tablespoons pure maple syrup

Vegetable oil, for brushing

PECAN PANCAKES

1-1/4 cups buttermilk

2 tablespoons unsalted butter, melted

1 egg

1 teaspoon vanilla extract

1 cup unbleached all-purpose flour

1/2 teaspoon baking soda

2 tablespoons granulated sugar

1/2 teaspoon salt

Confectioners' sugar, for dusting

1/4 cup chopped toasted pecans

To make the butter: In a blender or food processor, combine the butter and maple syrup. Transfer to a small dish, spreading the butter mixture evenly and smoothly to a thickness of approximately 1/4 inch. Cover with plastic wrap and refrigerate for 1 hour or overnight. When chilled, use a 1-inch heart-shaped aspic cutter to cut the chilled butter into hearts. Place on a chilled plate and keep refrigerated until ready to use.

Liberally brush heart-shaped pancake molds with oil. Place them in a nonstick skillet over medium heat to warm.

To make the pancakes: Preheat the oven to 200°F. In a blender, combine the buttermilk, melted butter, egg, and vanilla. Add the flour, baking soda, sugar, and salt and blend just until the dry ingredients are moistened. Pour enough batter into each of the heart molds to completely fill the mold. If necessary, gently tilt the pan when filling to help the batter spread and fill evenly. Cook for 2 to 3 minutes, until bubbles start to form and the edges of the hearts are slightly firm. Gently remove each mold and turn the pancakes to brown on the other side, about 1 minute longer. Transfer the pancakes to a warm serving platter in the oven until ready to serve. Clean and brush oil on the pancake molds before reusing, and repeat the process until all the batter is gone.

Remove the pancakes from the oven and dust with confectioners' sugar. Place half of the maple-butter hearts on the pancakes, sprinkle with pecans, and serve at once. Serve the remaining butter hearts on the side. *Makes eight 5-inch pancakes*

Buckwheat Crêpes with Strawberry-Balsamic Sauce

THESE CRÊPES ARE A ROMANTIC DESSERT OR BRUNCH DISH. THEY CAN BE MADE AHEAD
AND STACKED BETWEEN LAYERS OF PARCHMENT PAPER.

BUCKWHEAT CRÊPES

2/3 cup unbleached all-purpose flour

1/3 cup buckwheat flour

1 tablespoon sugar

Pinch of salt

3 eggs

1 cup milk

1/4 cup (1/2 stick) unsalted butter, melted

Clarified butter, for brushing

FILLING

1 cup sliced strawberries, 4 perfect slices reserved for garnish

1 cup heavy cream whipped with
2 tablespoons confectioners' sugar

STRAWBERRY-BALSAMIC SAUCE

1/4 cup balsamic vinegar

1 cup apple juice

1/2 cup sugar

1/2 teaspoon grated orange zest

1 teaspoon vanilla extract

1 pint strawberries, stemmed and halved

3 tablespoons unsalted butter

To make the crêpes: Combine the flours, sugar, and salt in a large mixing bowl. In another bowl, mix together the eggs, milk, and melted butter. Gradually add the flour mixture to the wet ingredients, whisking until smooth.

Heat a 6-inch crêpe pan over medium-high heat. Brush lightly with clarified butter. Ladle 3 tablespoons of the batter into the pan and tip to spread thin. Cook for 20 to 30 seconds on each side, until golden. Transfer to parchment paper to cool. Repeat with the remaining batter, stacking cooled crêpes between pieces of parchment until ready to use.

To make the filling: Place the sliced strawberries in a mixing bowl. Gently fold in half of the whipped cream and set aside.

To make the sauce: In a saucepan, combine the balsamic vinegar, apple juice, sugar, orange zest, and vanilla. Bring to a boil, stirring to dissolve the sugar. Add the halved strawberries and decrease the heat to low to achieve a simmer. Cook for 8 to 10 minutes, until the strawberries are softened. Stir in the butter and simmer until melted. Serve warm or at room temperature.

To assemble the crêpes: Spoon a generous amount of filling into each crêpe. Fold up one end and fold in the sides. Place seam-side down on individual serving plates, with one end open. (Some of the filling may spill out the open end.) Spoon some sauce on the plate. Garnish with a dollop of the remaining whipped cream topped with a reserved strawberry slice. *Serves 4*

Heart-Shaped French Toast Napoleons with Strawberry—Cream Cheese Filling

USE THREE SIZES (2-INCH, 3-INCH, AND 4-INCH) OF HEART-SHAPED COOKIE CUTTERS, LAYERING FROM LARGE ON THE BOTTOM TO SMALLEST ON TOP. OR CUT ALL OF THE HEARTS THE SAME SIZE AND STACK IN A MORE TRADITIONAL NAPOLEON.

12 ounces cream cheese

3 tablespoons confectioners' sugar

3 tablespoons strawberry jam

8 eggs

3/4 cup milk

1 tablespoon granulated sugar

1-1/2 teaspoons almond extract

Pinch of salt

18 slices brioche

Melted butter, for brushing

6 strawberries, stemmed, sliced, and fanned for garnish

With a mixer, whip together the cream cheese and confectioners' sugar. Add the strawberry jam and mix well. Refrigerate until ready to use.

In a flat dish, whisk together the eggs, milk, sugar, almond extract, and salt. Using heart-shaped cookie cutters, cut the brioche into 6 large, 6 medium, and 6 small hearts. One by one, place the hearts in the dish to soak up the egg mixture, spooning some on top to coat both sides well.

Heat a nonstick pan over medium heat and brush with butter. With a spatula, gently transfer the hearts to the pan and cook for 3 minutes on each side, until golden brown. Transfer to a tray in a warm oven and repeat with the remaining hearts.

Assemble the layers of French toast with a spoonful of the cream cheese mixture between each layer. Top with the remaining cream cheese and a strawberry fan. Serve at once. *Serves 6*

Rose Cup Fruit Sorbets

FOR A STUNNING PRESENTATION, USE A FRESH UNSPRAYED ROSE TO FRAME
A SCOOP OF SORBET. GENTLY REMOVE THE CENTER STAMEN AND HAVE A HELPER HOLD
THE PETALS OPEN AS YOU PUT THE SCOOP OF SORBET IN THE CENTER.

RASPBERRY-ORANGE SORBET

3/4 cup sugar

1/2 cup freshly squeezed orange juice

3 cups ripe raspberries

PLUM SORBET

1 pound ripe plums, peeled and seeded (about 2 cups)

1 cup spring water

1/2 cup sugar

To make the raspberry-orange sorbet: In a saucepan over medium heat, combine the sugar and orange juice and stir until the sugar dissolves. Set aside to cool.

Purée the raspberries in a blender or food processor. This should yield approximately 2 cups of raspberry purée. Stir the raspberry purée into the cooled sugar syrup and chill well.

Transfer to a chilled ice cream maker and freeze according to the manufacturer's directions.

To make the plum sorbet: Combine the plums, water, and sugar in a blender and process until smooth. Chill thoroughly.

Transfer to a chilled ice cream maker and freeze according to the manufacturer's directions. *Serves 8*

Tropical Fruit Valentine Punch

FOR A FRUITIER PUNCH, ADD SOME SLICES OF MANGO AND BANANA.

BLOOD-ORANGE JUICE ALSO MAKES A FESTIVE SUBSTITUTE FOR THE CRANBERRY JUICE.

1 cup sugar

1/2 cup water

4 cups cranberry juice

2 vanilla beans, split lengthwise

1 liter champagne, chilled

2 blood oranges, sliced 1/8 inch thick,
for garnish

2 star fruit, peeled and sliced
1/2 inch thick, for garnish

In a saucepan over medium heat, combine the sugar and water and stir constantly until the sugar is dissolved. Remove from the heat to cool. When cooled, transfer to a large glass bowl and add the cranberry juice and vanilla beans.

Refrigerate for at least 3 hours. Remove the vanilla beans, add the champagne, and garnish with blood orange and star fruit slices. Serve chilled. *Serves 6 to 8*

Valentine Margaritas

BEGIN YOUR NEXT ROMANTIC EVENING FOR TWO WITH THESE COLORFUL MARGARITAS.

YOU CAN MAKE THEM STRAIGHT UP AS SHOWN OR FROZEN AS DIRECTED BELOW.

1/2 cup guava nectar

1/4 cup cranberry juice

Coarse-grained red sugar for sugaring glass rim
(available at grocery stores)

1 lime

1/3 cup excellent-quality light or
white tequila, chilled

2 tablespoons freshly squeezed lime juice

Cointreau (optional)

In a mixing bowl, combine the guava nectar and cranberry juice and chill well.

Place the red sugar in a narrow, deep bowl. With a vegetable peeler, remove 2 strips of lime zest and set aside. Cut the lime into wedges. Swipe the rims of 2 glasses with a lime wedge and dip the wet edge of the glass into the red sugar. Gently shake off the excess sugar and set aside to dry.

Pour the tequila and lime juice into the sugar-rimmed glasses. Add the guava-cranberry mixture and a splash of Cointreau. Garnish each glass with a strip of lime zest.

For a slushy version, combine the guava nectar and cranberry juice and pour into an ice cube tray. Freeze until firm, then place the cubes in a blender with the tequila and lime juice, and purée on high until the mixture is smooth. *Serves 2*

gifts from the heart

Love Bug Valentines

THESE COLORFUL VALENTINE BUGS ARE FUN TO MAKE AND EASY
FOR YOUNG CHILDREN TO ASSEMBLE USING PRECUT SHAPES.
GIVE THEM LOTS OF HEART AND CIRCLE SIZES AND COLORS TO
EXPERIMENT WITH AND WATCH THEIR IMAGINATIONS RUN WILD.

YOU WILL NEED:

Colored paper

Pencil

Scissors

Heart and circle templates of varying sizes or stencil film
(available at craft supply stores)

Ruler

X-acto art knife

Glue stick

1/8-inch and 1/4-inch circle hand punches

White "gel" pen (available at craft and office supply stores)

5 by 7-inch envelopes

TO MAKE:

Trace various circle and heart shapes onto colored paper with a
pencil and cut them out with scissors. Using a ruler and X-acto
knife, cut 1/16 by 11-inch strips of black paper for the antennae.

For the ladybug, we used a 4-1/2-inch-diameter circle for the
body; a 1-1/4-inch-diameter circle for the head; and a 5-inch-wide
heart for the wings. For the butterfly, we used a pair of 3-inch-wide
hearts for the upper wings; a pair of 2-inch-wide hearts for the
lower wings; a 1-inch-wide heart for the head; and two pairs of
3/4-inch-wide hearts for the wing spots.

To assemble the ladybug: Using a glue stick, glue the head
onto the body leaving 1/2 inch of overhang on the head. Punch
out 2 eyeholes using the 1/8-inch circle hand punch and draw a
small mouth below the eyes with the white "gel" pen.

Using a 3-inch length of the black antennae paper, fold the
strip into a wide V and glue to the back side of the upper head,
making sure not to cover the eyeholes.

Fold the heart wings in half lengthwise. Using a 1/4-inch
circle hand punch, punch out spots in a random pattern on the
wings. Apply lots of glue to the folded edge of the paper wings and
attach the wings to the body below the head. Write a valentine
message on the back of the body with the white pen and insert it
into an envelope.

To assemble the butterfly: Using a glue stick, glue the wing
spots onto the center of each heart wing. Glue the top wings together at their tips, overlapping 1/4 inch and aligning the straight
sides of each heart wing along the bottom. Glue the bottom wings
together in the same manner, but align the straight sides of the
wings along the top. Apply a 1/8-inch strip of glue along the top of
the bottom wings and attach to the top wings overlapping 1/8 inch.

Punch out 2 eyeholes in the head heart. Using a 4-inch length
of the black antennae paper, fold the strip into a narrow V and glue
to the back of the head. Apply glue to the back of the head and to
1/4 inch of the lower antennae, and attach the head and antennae
to the wings in the upper center of the wingspread. When the glue
is dry, write a valentine message on the back of the wings. Turn the
butterfly over with the front facing toward you and gently fold the
wings in half vertically. Insert the finished butterfly into an envelope.

Hand-Stamped Valentines

NOTHING BRINGS A SMILE TO YOUR LOVED ONE'S FACE FASTER THAN A BEAUTIFUL HANDMADE VALENTINE.

THIS SIMPLE ASSORTMENT OF UNIQUE CARDS WAS CREATED USING BOTH HANDMADE AND READY-MADE RUBBER STAMPS.

HANDMADE STAMPS ARE EASY TO MAKE USING ADHESIVE-BACKED FOAM PADS AFFIXED TO WOODEN BLOCKS.

YOU CAN CREATE A WONDERFUL VARIETY OF STAMPING EFFECTS BY VARYING THE AMOUNT OF INK AND PRESSURE USED.

YOU WILL NEED:

Pencil

1/8-inch-thick adhesive-backed foam stamp pads (available at art and craft supply stores)

Scissors

Wooden blocks in various sizes

Colored inkpads

White paper for experimenting with stamps

Textured card stock or blank note cards with envelopes

Ruler

X-acto art knife

Glue stick

Rubber stamp letter kits

1/8-inch hole punch

Decorative ribbons

Pens

TO MAKE:

Using a pencil, draw 2 hearts on the paper side of the adhesive-backed foam. Cut out the hearts using scissors, remove the paper backing, and adhere the hearts to the centers of the wooden blocks.

Press the stamps in ink and experiment on white paper, varying the amount of ink and pressure. To create fading hearts, press a heart in ink only one time and make a row of hearts. Each heart will be slightly lighter than the one before it.

To make a hand-stamped photo-frame valentine, cut out a piece of paper that is twice as large as the final size you want your card to be. Fold it in half and cut out a window slightly smaller than your photo from the top side of the card, using a ruler and X-acto knife. Glue a photo inside the card under the window frame with a glue stick. Stamp a decorative border around the outer frame with your ready-made and handmade stamps. Using a hole punch, punch 1/8-inch holes on the front and back right edge of the card and thread a ribbon through the holes to make a bow closure.

To make a heart-shaped poem valentine, write your poem on the top side of the card or print it out using a personal computer and laser printer. Hand-stamp over your poem using lighter color ink.

To make a hand-stamped valentine bookmark, cut out a strip of heavyweight card stock 1 by 8 inches. Stamp a decorative design on the strip and write a valentine message over the stamping with a dark color pen. Punch a 1/8-inch hole at the bottom center of the strip and thread a 12-inch length of 1/8-inch-wide satin ribbon through the hole. Present inside a favorite love story or book of poems.

... True love is a durable fire
In the mind ever burning;
Never sick, never old,
From itself never turning ...

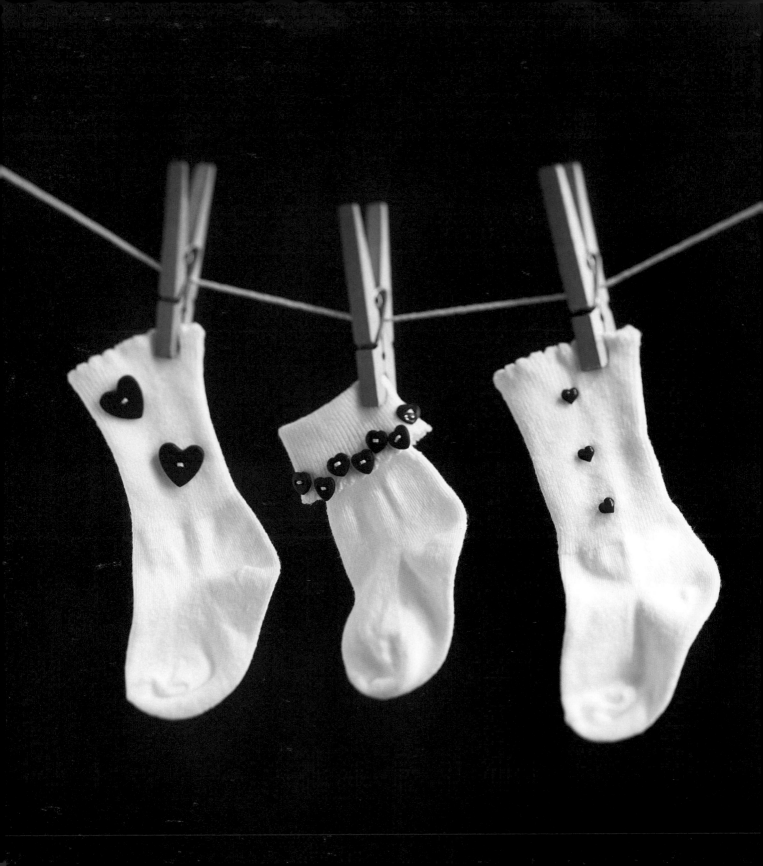

Heart-Button Baby Socks

THESE WHIMSICAL BABY SOCKS ARE EASY TO CREATE WITH HEART-SHAPED BUTTONS

OF DIFFERENT SIZES. THEY MAKE A CUTE FIRST BIRTHDAY OR BABY SHOWER GIFT FOR A FEBRUARY BABY.

TODDLERS WILL ENJOY THEM, TOO, TO MARK THE OCCASION OF THEIR FIRST VALENTINE'S DAY.

YOU WILL NEED:

Assorted sizes of red heart-shaped buttons
(available at fabric and craft supply stores)

Pairs of cotton baby socks

Pencil

Thread

Needle

Small sewing scissors

TO MAKE:

Place the buttons on flattened socks in the desired design. Mark the placement of each button with a small pencil mark.

Sew each button in place by hand using needle and doubled thread. Buttons placed in a clustered design can be stitched in place with a continuous chain of stitches on the underside of the sock cuff. Repeat the design on the other sock and stitch buttons in place.

NOTE: Socks should be hand-washed.

Heart Soaps

THESE DELICATE PASTEL GLYCERIN SOAPS MAKE LOVELY VALENTINE GIFTS FOR FRIENDS OR CO-WORKERS. SELECT SEVERAL SHADES OF PALE PINK GLYCERIN, AND ADD YOUR FRIEND'S FAVORITE FRAGRANCE.

YOU WILL NEED:

Glycerin blocks in assorted colors

Heart-shaped loaf soap mold
(available at craft supply stores)

2-cup Pyrex glass measuring cup

Essential oil fragrances
(optional; available at craft supply stores)

Spoon

Knife

Nylon stocking

TO MAKE:

Estimate how much glycerin you will need for the mold you are using by comparing the volume of the glycerin block to the capacity of the mold. On a clean surface, cut the glycerin into 1/2-inch chunks.

Place a loaf cylinder securely on its base on a level work surface. Melt a small amount of glycerin in the measuring cup in a microwave for 15 seconds and fill the loaf mold 1/2 inch full. Let cool completely in the refrigerator to seal the mold to the base, approximately 1 hour.

When ready to fill the rest of mold, place more glycerin chunks into the measuring cup and begin to melt in the microwave for 15 seconds. Add a few drops of fragrance oil. Continue heating in 5-second increments until the glycerin is melted. Do not overheat or boil. Let cool for 30 seconds, until a film forms on the surface of the liquid. Use a spoon to scoop away the film and any foam that has formed on the surface. Fill the mold to the desired height. Let cool for at least 2 hours in the refrigerator, remove the base from the cylinder, and push the loaf of soap gently out of the mold.

With a large, sharp kitchen knife, slice the loaf into individual soaps of desired widths. Gently buff any rough edges with a nylon stocking.

63

savory hearts

6

Parmesan Braided Hearts

FOR THE BEST RESULTS, FROZEN PUFF PASTRY SHOULD BE THAWED IN ITS PACKAGE BEFORE USING AND CHILLED BEFORE BAKING.

YOU CAN ALSO TRY POPPYSEEDS IN PLACE OF THE SESAME SEEDS, IF DESIRED.

1 package (2 sheets 9-1/2 by 10 inches)
frozen puff pastry, defrosted

1-1/2 cups (6 ounces) finely grated Parmigiano-Reggiano cheese

1/4 cup sesame seeds

2 tablespoons freshly ground black pepper

1 teaspoon salt

2 eggs, beaten

Preheat the oven to 425°F. Line a baking sheet with parchment paper. Place the puff pastry sheets on a lightly floured work surface. With a sharp knife, cut each sheet crosswise into 1/2-inch-wide strips and roll each strip into a cylinder approximately 9-1/2 inches long. Each sheet of pastry will yield 18 cylinders.

In a shallow dish, combine the cheese, sesame seeds, pepper, and salt. Dip each puff pastry cylinder into the egg, then dredge in the cheese mixture. Set aside on a floured work surface until all of the cylinders are coated. Put the ends of 3 cylinders together and pinch tightly. Braid, then shape into a heart. Pinch the end to secure. Repeat with the remaining puff pastry. Place each heart on the prepared baking sheet and refrigerate for 20 to 30 minutes.

Bake the braided hearts for 8 to 10 minutes, or until golden brown. *Makes 12 hearts*

Spicy Red Pizzette with Tomatoes, Red Peppers, and Red Onion

TO PIERCE THESE HEARTS WITH CUPID'S ARROW, STRIP SOME OF THE LEAVES FROM THE LOWER STEM OF
AN 8-INCH SPRIG OF ROSEMARY, THEN INSERT IT DIAGONALLY INTO THE BAKED PIZZETTE.

1 envelope active dry yeast

2 tablespoons sugar

1-1/2 cups warm (105°–115°F) water

3-1/2 cups unbleached all-purpose flour

1/2 cup semolina

1 tablespoon salt

3 tablespoons olive oil, plus extra for brushing pizzas

4 ounces part skim mozzarella cheese, grated

3 plum tomatoes, diced

1 red pepper, roasted, peeled, and julienned

1 red onion, diced

2 teaspoons minced rosemary

Crushed red pepper flakes

In a small bowl, dissolve the yeast and sugar in the water. Let stand until foamy, about 5 minutes.

In a heavy-duty electric mixer with bread hook (or by hand), combine the flour, semolina, and salt. Add the yeast mixture and olive oil. Work into the flour mixture until the dough is smooth. Turn the dough out onto a lightly floured work surface and knead until smooth and not sticky. Shape into a ball and place in a lightly oiled bowl. Cover and let rest for 30 minutes until doubled in volume.

Punch the dough down. Using a rolling pin, roll out the dough to a thickness of 1/2 inch. With an elongated 7 by 4-inch heart-shaped cookie cutter, cut out pizzette hearts and place on a lightly floured baking sheet. Gather the dough scraps and roll and cut out more pizzette until all of the dough is used. Let the hearts rest, covered, for 15 minutes.

Place a pizza stone in the oven and preheat to 450°F.

With your fingertips, flatten the center of the hearts, leaving a 1/4-inch edge. Brush the center with a little olive oil. Sprinkle a little mozzarella cheese onto each pizza. Arrange some diced tomato, red pepper, and onion on top. Sprinkle with a pinch of rosemary and pepper flakes to taste. Bake for 8 to 10 minutes on the pizza stone, until the dough is firm and lightly browned.

Makes 18 pizzette

Heart-Shaped Blini with Red Caviar Crème Fraîche

THESE FREE-FORM HEART-SHAPED BLINI ARE EASY TO CREATE USING A LARGE PLASTIC SQUEEZE BOTTLE TO HOLD THE BATTER.

BE SURE TO CUT OFF THE TIP SO THAT THE BATTER CAN PASS THROUGH AN OPENING THAT IS AT LEAST 1/8 INCH IN DIAMETER.

1 cup crème fraîche

1/4 cup (1/2 stick) unsalted butter,
at room temperature

4 tablespoons salmon roe, plus 1 tablespoon for garnish

1 shallot, finely minced

Freshly ground black pepper

1 envelope active dry yeast

1-1/4 cups lukewarm milk

1 teaspoon sugar

1/4 cup buckwheat flour

1 cup unbleached all-purpose flour

2 egg yolks, lightly beaten

1 tablespoon melted unsalted butter, plus extra
for brushing

2 teaspoons sour cream

2 egg whites

2 hard-boiled eggs, sliced crosswise 1/4 inch thick

Flat-leaf parsley leaves, for garnish

In a mixing bowl, combine the crème fraîche, butter, salmon roe, and shallot, and season with pepper to taste. Place in a pastry bag with a large star tip and refrigerate.

In a large mixing bowl, combine the yeast, milk, and sugar. Stir until the yeast and sugar have dissolved. Add the buckwheat flour, all-purpose flour, and egg yolks. Mix well until smooth. Cover and let rise in a warm, draft-free place until doubled in volume, about 1-1/2 hours. Punch down the batter and add the melted butter and sour cream. Beat the egg whites until stiff and fold into the batter. Place the batter in a plastic squeeze bottle.

Heat a nonstick skillet over medium heat and brush with butter. With the squeeze bottle, outline the shape of a 2-inch heart, then fill in with a spiral motion. Cook for about 2 minutes on each side, until lightly browned. Transfer to a platter and keep warm until ready to serve.

Place a slice of hard-boiled egg on each blini. Pipe the salmon roe mixture onto the egg and garnish with the reserved roe and a leaf of parsley. *Makes six 4-inch blini*

Mini Heart Frittatas

THIS IS AN EASY PARTY TREAT. YOU CAN MAKE THEM A HALF DAY AHEAD, THEN REHEAT IN AN OVEN FOR 10 MINUTES AT 350°F JUST BEFORE SERVING. A SMALL PAPER DOILY MAKES A FESTIVE SERVING NAPKIN FOR THE INDIVIDUAL FRITTATAS.

2 tablespoons olive oil

1/4 cup finely diced onion

4 asparagus tips

1/4 cup finely diced red bell pepper,
plus 1 tablespoon for garnish

3 tablespoons grated Gruyère cheese

1 tablespoon minced fresh flat-leaf parsley,
plus 1 tablespoon for garnish

2 eggs, lightly beaten

Salt and freshly ground black pepper

1/4 cup grated Parmigiano-Reggiano cheese

1 tablespoon finely minced chives, for garnish

Preheat the oven to 375°F. Lightly oil a 12-cavity heart-shaped mini muffin pan.

In a sauté pan, heat 1 tablespoon of the olive oil over medium heat. Add the onion and sauté for 2 minutes, until softened, but not browned. Add the asparagus tips and sauté for about 2 to 3 minutes, until softened. Transfer to a small dish and set aside. In the same pan, heat the remaining 1 tablespoon oil, add the pepper, and sauté for 3 minutes, until softened. Spoon the onion-asparagus mixture into 4 muffin cups, distributing 1 asparagus tip into each cup; spoon the red pepper into 4 muffin cups; and distribute the grated Gruyère into the remaining 4 muffin cups.

In a 2-cup Pyrex measuring cup, combine the parsley and eggs. Season with salt and pepper to taste and carefully pour into the muffin cups. Sprinkle Parmigiano-Reggiano on top and bake for about 6 minutes, until a toothpick inserted in the center of a heart comes out clean. Garnish with diced red pepper, minced parsley, and minced chives. Serve hot at once or later at room temperature. *Makes 12 mini frittatas*

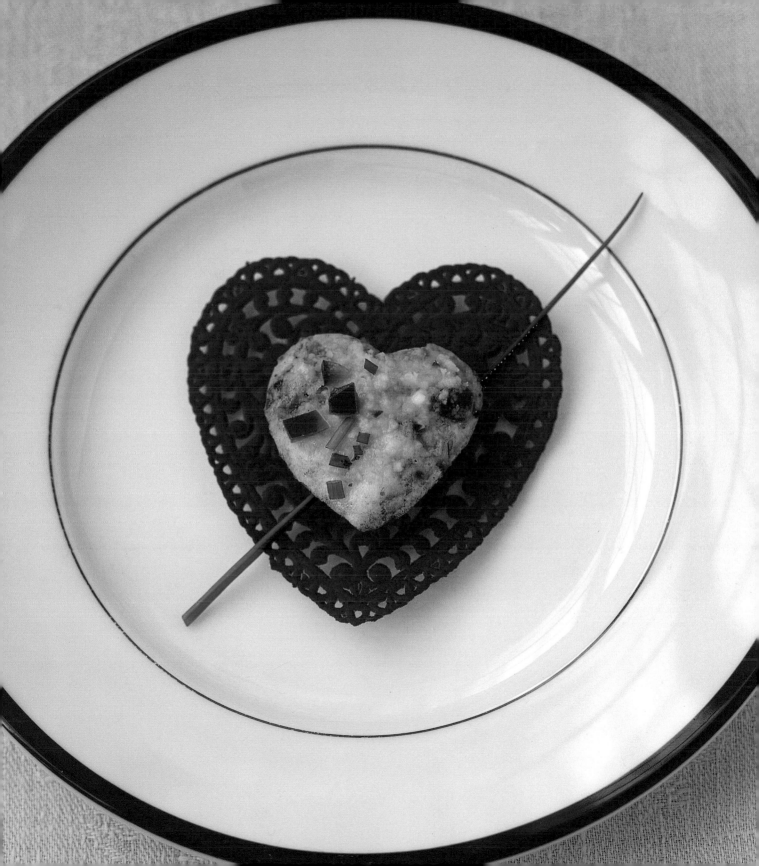

Belgian Endive with Red Pepper–Cream Cheese Filling

IN THIS COLORFUL APPETIZER, RED PEPPERS ARE USED FOR BOTH THE FILLING AND THE FESTIVE HEART-SHAPED GARNISH.

IF YOU ARE SHORT ON TIME, YOU CAN USE CANNED PRE-ROASTED PEPPERS FOR THE FILLING.

2 red bell peppers

8 ounces goat cheese

2 tablespoons salt-cured capers, rinsed and drained

Salt and freshly ground black pepper

2 heads Belgian endive, separated into spears

Cut 4 large flat slices from the sides of 1 red pepper, removing the seeds and membranes. With a heart-shaped aspic cutter, cut out little hearts and set aside. Roast the remaining red pepper over an open flame until charred (see note). Place in a brown paper bag to cool. When cooled, remove the skin and seeds. In a food processor, purée the goat cheese, capers, and roasted pepper until smooth. Season with salt and pepper to taste. Place in a pastry bag fitted with a medium star tip and refrigerate until ready to serve. Pipe the filling onto each spear of endive. Garnish with the red pepper hearts. *Serves 6*

NOTE: The red pepper can also be roasted under a broiler. Just place it on a baking sheet and broil, turning occasionally, for 3 to 4 minutes, until darkened.

Red Beet and Red Chard Risotto

THE AVAILABILITY OF HEIRLOOM VARIETIES OF BEETS HAS PROVIDED US WITH NEW CHOICES, SUCH AS

THE STRIPED BABY BEET. EQUALLY ROMANTIC IS THE TRADITIONAL SWEET BABY RED BEET.

2 bunches (about 15) small beets

6 tablespoons extra virgin olive oil

Salt and freshly ground black pepper

4 to 5 cups chicken stock, heated

1/2 cup chopped onion

2 ounces pancetta, chopped

1 pound ruby red chard, washed and julienned

3 cups arborio or carnaroli rice

1 cup dry white wine, at room temperature

2 tablespoons unsalted butter

Preheat the oven to 400°F. Lightly oil a medium casserole.

In a large saucepan, bring 3 cups of salted water to a boil. Select 6 of the smallest and prettiest baby beets for garnish and set aside. Trim the roots and stems from the remaining beets, scrub well, and quarter them lengthwise. Drop the quartered beets into the boiling water and cook for 8 to 12 minutes, until fork tender. Drain, reserving the water, and remove the skins. Place the beets in the prepared casserole and drizzle with 2 tablespoons of the olive oil. Season with salt and pepper to taste. Roast in the oven for about 20 minutes, until lightly browned. Set aside.

Strain the reserved beet cooking water and combine it with the stock in a large saucepan over medium heat. Bring to a simmer.

In another large heavy saucepan over medium heat, heat the remaining 4 tablespoons olive oil. Add the onion and pancetta and cook for 5 minutes, until the onion is golden brown. Add the chard and cook for 4 to 5 minutes, until softened. With a slotted spoon, remove the chard mixture and set aside. In the same pan, add the rice and stir for 3 to 4 minutes, until all the grains are well coated and the rice is translucent. Add the wine and stir until it is completely absorbed.

Begin to add the simmering beet stock, 1/2 cup at a time, stirring frequently to prevent sticking. Wait until the stock is almost completely absorbed (but never dry on top) before adding the next 1/2 cup, reserving about 1/4 cup to add at the end. Stir for 18 to 20 minutes.

When the rice is tender, but still firm, turn off the heat and stir in the quartered beets, chard, butter, and the remaining stock. Season with salt and pepper, garnish with reserved whole beets, and serve at once. *Serves 6*

Salad of Beets, Artichoke Hearts, and Hearts of Palm

A HEARTFUL SALAD, THIS RECIPE IS BEST MADE AT LEAST 2 HOURS IN ADVANCE,

TO ALLOW THE INGREDIENTS TO ABSORB SOME OF THE VINAIGRETTE.

3 large beets

1 (12-ounce) can hearts of palm, drained and sliced crosswise 1/4 inch thick

1/2 cup artichoke hearts (packed in oil), drained

1/2 cup freshly squeezed lemon juice

3/4 cup safflower oil

1 teaspoon finely grated lemon zest

1 bunch chives, minced

Salt and freshly ground white pepper

Bring a saucepan of water to a boil. Trim the roots and stems from the beets and scrub well. Drop into the boiling water and cook for 15 minutes, or until fork tender. Drain and remove the skins. Slice the beets into 1/4-inch-thick slices. Cut into heart shapes with a 1-inch heart-shaped cookie cutter.

In a large bowl, combine the beet hearts, hearts of palm, and artichoke hearts. Toss to mix well.

Place the lemon juice in a small mixing bowl. While continuously whisking, slowly drizzle in the oil. Stir in the lemon zest and chives and season with salt and pepper to taste. Toss with the salad and serve at once or refrigerate until ready to serve. *Serves 6*

Grilled Parmesan Polenta Hearts with Goat Cheese Sauce

THESE SAVORY POLENTA HEARTS MAKE A WONDERFUL APPETIZER OR ACCOMPANIMENT TO ROAST CHICKEN OR PORK. THE RECIPE CAN BE EASILY ADAPTED TO AN HORS D'OEUVRE BY USING A SMALLER 1-1/2-INCH COOKIE CUTTER AND A THICKER GOAT CHEESE MIXTURE. USE ONLY 1/2 CUP OF HEAVY CREAM TO MAKE A SPREADABLE GOAT CHEESE TOPPING.

4-1/2 cups chicken stock

1-1/2 cups polenta

1/2 cup dry white wine

2 cloves garlic, finely chopped

2 cups heavy cream

5 ounces goat cheese

2 teaspoons fresh minced thyme

Salt and freshly ground black pepper

4 oil-packed sundried tomatoes, julienned, for garnish

Preheat a grill. Lightly oil a baking sheet. Preheat the oven to 350°F.

In a large saucepan over high heat, bring the chicken stock to a boil. Gradually whisk in the polenta, whisking constantly. Decrease the heat to medium and cook, stirring constantly, for about 20 minutes, or until the polenta thickens and comes easily away from the side of the pan. Spread the polenta evenly onto the prepared baking sheet, smooth the top, and bake for 15 minutes, until lightly browned. Set aside to cool.

Combine the wine and garlic in a saucepan over medium heat and boil for about 5 minutes, until reduced by half. Whisk in the cream, goat cheese, and thyme and heat through. Season with salt and pepper to taste. Keep warm.

With a 3-inch heart-shaped cookie cutter, cut out hearts from the polenta. With a metal spatula, transfer the hearts to a plate until ready to grill. Grill for 3 to 4 minutes on each side, until heated through. To serve, spoon 2 tablespoons of the warm goat cheese sauce onto 8 small plates. Top with a hot polenta heart and garnish with sundried tomatoes. *Serves 8*

Heart-Shaped Ravioli with Creamy Pesto Sauce

PINE NUTS HAVE AN ANCIENT HISTORY OF INDUCING LOVE. USE THIS RECIPE WITH CARE!

PESTO SAUCE

2 cloves garlic, peeled

1/2 cup packed fresh basil leaves

3 tablespoons pine nuts, toasted

3 tablespoons extra virgin olive oil

2 tablespoons finely grated Parmigiano-Reggiano cheese

2 cups heavy cream

Salt and freshly ground black pepper

RAVIOLI

1 cup fresh ricotta cheese

3 tablespoons chopped fresh flat-leaf parsley

Salt and freshly ground black pepper

3 cups unbleached all-purpose flour

3 eggs

3 tablespoons tomato paste

1 tablespoon olive oil

To make the pesto: With a food processor running, drop in the garlic. Add the basil and pine nuts and process to a grainy texture. With the machine running, gradually add the olive oil to the desired consistency. Fold in the cheese by hand.

To make the ravioli: In a small bowl, combine the ricotta and parsley and season with salt and pepper to taste. Set aside.

Place the flour in a food processor fitted with the steel knife blade. In a small container with a pour spout, whisk the eggs with the tomato paste and oil. With the processor running, slowly add the egg mixture to the flour until the dough starts to come away from the sides of the work bowl. Process for 30 seconds and check the consistency. The dough should be moist enough to pinch together, but not sticky. On a lightly floured work surface, knead the dough to form a ball. Place in a plastic bag to rest for 15 minutes. Roll out one-fourth of the dough at a time, keeping the remaining dough in the plastic bag to avoid drying it out.

Using a hand-cranked pasta maker, start on the widest setting. Pass the pasta through 8 to 10 times, folding it in half each time, until the dough is smooth. If the dough tears, it may be too wet; dust it with flour, brushing off the excess. Using a narrower setting each time, continue putting the dough through the rollers without folding it, until the dough is the desired thickness. With a cookie cutter, cut heart shapes. While still moist, place a small amount of the filling mixture on the center of a heart. Top with another heart, pressing the edges together with a fork to seal. Set aside on a lightly floured tray while you make the rest of the ravioli in the same way.

In a saucepan over medium heat, warm the cream. Add the pesto and season with salt and pepper to taste. Keep warm.

Bring salted water to a boil in a large saucepan. Cook the pasta hearts in the water for 1 to 2 minutes, until tender. Drain and toss with the pesto sauce. Serve at once. *Serves 6*

decorative hearts

7

Pepper Berry Heart Wreath

DRIED PEPPER BERRIES ARE WIDELY AVAILABLE AND
ARE THE PERFECT PINK COLOR FOR A VALENTINE'S DAY
WREATH. IF HUNG AND LATER STORED IN A DRY PLACE,
YOUR WREATH SHOULD LAST SEVERAL SEASONS.

YOU WILL NEED:

Quick-drying light-red spray paint

9- or 10-inch heart-shaped willow wreath frame
(available at craft supply stores)

Hot glue gun with glue sticks

1 large bouquet dried pepper berries
(available at florists and craft supply stores)

24-inch length of wide satin ribbon

2 dried pink roses

TO MAKE:

Lightly spray paint a wreath frame on all sides and let dry.

Heat a hot glue gun containing a glue stick. Starting at the top of the wreath frame, begin inserting little sprigs of pepper berries into the crevasses of the frame and secure with a drop of hot glue. Layer sprigs on top of each other moving down and around the frame in one direction on each side. Note: Hot gluing will be less messy if you apply the glue to the berry sprigs before inserting them into the frame.

Cover the frame entirely so that none of the top surface of the frame shows through the berries. You can fill in cracks with very small berry clusters at the end as needed.

Thread the ribbon through the top back of the frame and tie in a bow to hang. For an added touch, insert 2 dried pink roses at the top center of the wreath.

Let's

a

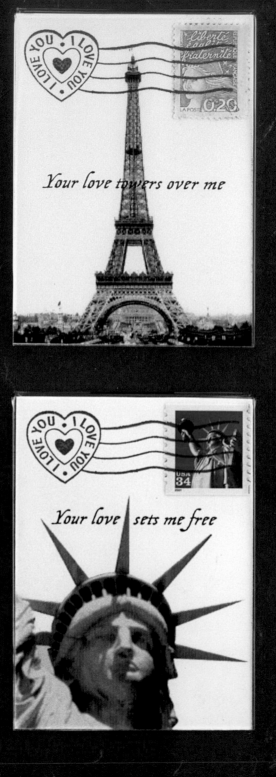

I LOVE YOU · I LOVE YOU

Your love towers over me

I LOVE YOU · I LOVE YOU

Your love sets me free

34

my

Love Note Magnets

THE IDEA FOR THESE LOVABLE MAGNETS CAME FROM A SPECIAL "I LOVE YOU" POSTMARK RUBBER STAMP
FOUND AT THE LOCAL OFFICE SUPPLY STORE. YOU CAN USE ANY THEME AS YOUR INSPIRATION, BUT HERE WE USED
OLD POSTCARDS, POSTAGE STAMPS, AND CLIP ART IMAGES TO CREATE A VARIETY OF "LOVE NOTES."

YOU WILL NEED:

Clip art books, postcards,
postage stamps, typography books,
rubber postmark stamp

Acrylic magnet frames in various sizes
(available at office and
craft supply stores)

Pencil

Tracing paper

Scissors

Glue stick

Red inkpad

Colored fine-tipped markers
or pencils

X-acto art knife

Ruler

Decorative-edge scissors

TO MAKE:

Decide on your magnet theme and make a few sketches or planning notes before assembling your artwork. For the postcard magnets, we made notes about possible cities and collected clip art, old postcards, and stamps to use as imagery. For the pictogram magnets, we listed valentine messages that could be created by letters, words, and pictures and then referred to clip art books to find the pictures we needed.

To create your layout templates, trace your magnet frames several times with a pencil onto tracing paper. Reduce your artwork to fit inside your templates, using a copy machine. Trim to fit inside the perimeter of your magnet tracing, and glue art into place on tracing paper using a glue stick. Alternately, if you have access to a scanner, personal computer, and ink-jet laser printer, you can scan your artwork and size and place it in a sized template using desktop publishing software.

Choose typefaces and borders you like from typography books or create them on your personal computer to cut out and glue on your template or arrange using desktop publishing software.

Once you have the artwork in place on the template, make a clean copy on a color or black-and-white copy machine or an ink-jet printer. Apply postage stamps, stamp with a rubber postmark stamp, and color any desired areas by hand, using markers or colored pencils.

Trim the finished art to fit with an X-acto knife and ruler or decorative-edge scissors and slide into the magnet frames. Wrap as a gift and give to your favorite valentine.

Sweetheart Picture Frame

THIS WHIMSICAL FRAME TAKES ITS INSPIRATION FROM THE CLASSIC CANDIES

THAT COME IN PASTEL COLORS PRINTED WITH PINK VALENTINE MESSAGES. IT TAKES ONLY MINUTES TO CREATE

AND MAKES A CHARMING GIFT FOR A NEW BABY OR SPECIAL GRANDPARENT.

BUY A BOX OF THE "MESSAGE" CANDIES TO USE AS A GUIDE WHEN HAND-LETTERING YOUR FRAME HEARTS.

YOU WILL NEED:

12 (1 by 1/8-inch) wooden hearts
(available at craft supply stores)

Acrylic craft paints in pastel colors
(available at craft supply stores)

1/4-inch soft-bristle craft paintbrush

Paper towels

Plastic water container and water

Red or dark pink fine-tipped marker

White store-bought picture frame

Craft glue

TO MAKE:

Lay the wooden hearts out on a clean work surface or paper towels. Paint the edges and topsides of all the hearts with acrylic paints. Let dry for 5 minutes; turn them over and paint the undersides and let dry completely. Be sure to rinse and dry the brush well when changing colors.

Using a fine-tipped marker, write different valentine messages on each heart using only capital letters. If you make a mistake, turn the heart over and write on the other side, or paint over with more craft paint.

Glue the hearts around the edges of the frame using craft glue and insert a favorite photograph.

Drawstring Heart Sachets

THESE FRAGRANT SACHETS, USED TO
SCENT DRAWERS, TRUNKS, OR CLOSETS, ARE LASTING
KEEPSAKES TO PRESENT TO FRIENDS AND RELATIVES
FOR VALENTINE'S DAY AND OTHER OCCASIONS.

YOU WILL NEED:

Scissors

Straight pins

1/4 yard of 36-inch wide red and white cotton gingham
or pink cotton chambray fabric

20-inch length of red jumbo (5/8 inch) rick rack

Red or pink sewing thread

Needle or sewing machine

Sewing scissors

1 yard of 1/4-inch red grosgrain ribbon

Safety pin

1-3/4 cups lavender petals per sachet
(available at craft supply stores)

ENLARGE BY 400%

TO MAKE:

Using a copy machine, enlarge the heart sachet pattern below by 400 percent to 6-3/4 inches wide. Cut out with scissors.

Pin the pattern to a double thickness of fabric and cut out sachet pieces.

Using large, 1/4-inch stitches, baste the rick rack to the heart edges of one piece of sachet with a needle and thread, making sure the edges of the rick rack overlap the fabric edge by 1/2 inch. Trim the ends of the rick rack with scissors.

Place the other piece of sachet cloth on top of the first half with the right sides facing each other. Starting at the upper curve of one side of the heart, sew the pieces together, 1/4 inch from the edges, by hand using very small stitches or by machine. Backstitch at the beginning and ends of the heart to secure the stitching near the drawstrings. Stop stitching when you reach the opposite end of the heart's curve. Do not sew the straight edges at the top center together.

Fold straight, top edges over 1/4 inch on both front and back pieces of cloth. Stitch down by hand close to raw edge leaving ends open for ribbon insertion.

Cut two 12-inch lengths of grosgrain ribbon. Using a safety pin attached to the ends of the ribbons, insert into each drawstring channel and pull through. Remove safety pin.

Turn the finished sachet right side out and knot each pair of ribbons together at their ends on either side of the sachet opening. Tie the remaining length of grosgrain ribbon into a bow and sew onto the front of the sachet if desired. Fill the sachet with lavender and pull the ribbon ends of the drawstrings to tightly close.

hearts for kids

Cookie-Cutter Heart Sandwiches

PACKAGING IS EVERYTHING TO KIDS. TUCKING A HEART-SHAPED SANDWICH
INTO YOUR CHILDREN'S LUNCH BOXES IS A GREAT WAY TO REMIND THEM YOU LOVE THEM
AND A CREATIVE WAY TO PACKAGE EVERY DAY LUNCH FAVORITES.

TURKEY AND CRANBERRY

Cut canned cranberry jelly into 1/2-inch-thick slices and layer it on
your favorite bread with thinly sliced turkey. Using a heart-shaped
cookie cutter, cut out each sandwich. You can also cut hearts from
the cranberry slices with an aspic cutter. Make an open-faced
sandwich with thinly sliced turkey and top with cranberry hearts.

SOME OTHER FUN SANDWICH IDEAS:

· Cream cheese and jelly, cut into hearts with a cookie cutter
· Open-faced peanut butter with banana hearts (cut with an
  aspic cutter)
· Ham and Swiss cheese, cut into hearts with a cookie cutter
· Heart-shaped pita breads or crackers topped with tuna salad
· Heart-shaped cucumber slices topped with cream cheese and
  a red pepper heart
· Grilled cheese, cut into hearts with a cookie cutter

Chocolate Heart Peppermint Ice Cream Sandwiches

A CHILD'S DELIGHT, THESE ARE PERFECT DO-AHEAD TREATS FOR A VALENTINE'S DAY PARTY.

1/2 cup (1 stick) unsalted butter,
at room temperature

1 teaspoon vanilla extract

2/3 cup firmly packed brown sugar

1/3 cup granulated sugar

Pinch of salt

1 egg

2 ounces bittersweet chocolate, melted

1-1/2 cups unbleached all-purpose flour

1 pint vanilla ice cream

1 teaspoon red food coloring

4 ounces peppermint candy, crushed

In a mixing bowl, cream together the butter, vanilla, brown sugar, and granulated sugar. When light and fluffy, stir in the salt, egg, and melted chocolate. Add the flour, mixing well. Shape into a flattened disk and refrigerate for at least 1 hour or overnight.

Preheat the oven to 400°F. Line a baking sheet with parchment paper. On a lightly floured work surface, roll the dough out to 1/4 inch thick. Using a 4-inch scalloped heart-shaped cookie cutter, cut 12 heart shapes. If desired, cut out a small 1-inch heart from the center of half of the large hearts. Transfer to the prepared baking sheet and bake for 8 to 9 minutes, until crisp. Set aside to cool on a wire rack.

Place the ice cream, food coloring, and peppermints in a food processor and pulse to blend in the candies. Transfer to a metal mixing bowl and freeze until firm enough to hold its shape, but soft enough to spread.

With a rubber spatula, spread a layer of ice cream on 6 heart cookies. Top each with another cookie. Serve at once, or place on a sheet pan to freeze to serve later. *Makes 6 sandwiches*

Valentine Candy Ice Pops

THESE FRUITY ICE POPS ARE AS FUN FOR KIDS TO MAKE AS THEY ARE TO EAT.
TRY OTHER BERRIES SUCH AS BLUEBERRIES OR RASPBERRIES FOR A COLORFUL VARIATION.

6 cups strawberries, stemmed

1/2 cup sugar

12 (3-ounce) paper cups or Popsicle molds

1/3 cup small (1/8-inch) heart-shaped
valentine candies

12 Popsicle sticks

In a blender, purée the strawberries with the sugar until smooth. Divide the mixture evenly among the paper cups. Freeze for about 20 minutes, until the mixture begins to set up. Drop in the candies, using a skewer to distribute them throughout the ice pops. Insert a Popsicle stick in each and continue to freeze the pops for about 30 minutes more, until firm. *Makes 12 pops*

Strawberry Heart Jigglers

WITH MOM'S HELP, THIS IS A DELIGHTFUL TREAT TO TAKE TO SCHOOL. USE A MINIATURE (1-INCH) ASPIC CUTTER FOR SHAPING THE STRAWBERRY HEARTS. FOR MORE VARIETY, CUT HEARTS FROM BANANA SLICES FOR SOME OF THE SQUARES.

1 cup freshly squeezed lemon juice, strained

1/2 cup sugar

4 packages unflavored gelatin

2 (12-ounce) cans lemon-lime soda

4 tablespoons grenadine

1 pint large ripe strawberries, stemmed and sliced lengthwise 1/8 inch thick

In a mixing bowl, combine the lemon juice and sugar, stirring until dissolved. Sprinkle the gelatin over the mixture and let stand for 2 to 3 minutes.

In a small saucepan over high heat, bring the soda to a boil. Add the gelatin mixture, stirring until the gelatin is completely dissolved. Pour half of the mixture into a bowl, the other half into a separate bowl. Add 1 tablespoon grenadine to 1 bowl, and 3 tablespoons grenadine to the other.

Pour about 3/4 cup of the mixture from each bowl into two separate 8-inch-square pans and place in the refrigerator to gel, about 20 minutes. Set aside the bowls with the remaining mixtures at room temperature.

Cut the strawberry slices into heart shapes using a 1-inch aspic cutter. Place the strawberry hearts spaced approximately 1 inch apart, across the thin layer of chilled gelatin, pressing lightly with your finger to embed them. Cover each with the remaining gelatin mixtures and chill until completely set, about 3 hours. Cut into 2-inch squares and serve on a white platter, alternating the squares by color in a checkerboard pattern. *Makes 32 squares*

Peanut Butter–Chocolate Hearts

THESE IRRESISTIBLE COOKIES ARE AS MUCH FUN FOR KIDS TO MAKE AS THEY ARE TO EAT. LET THEM CHOOSE
THEIR FAVORITE SPRINKLES TO DECORATE THESE DOUBLE-RICH CHOCOLATE–PEANUT BUTTER TREATS.

1/2 cup creamy unsalted peanut butter

3/4 cup sugar

1 egg

1/2 teaspoon vanilla extract

1 tablespoon heavy cream

1-1/2 cups unbleached all-purpose flour

1/8 teaspoon salt

1/4 teaspoon baking powder

1/3 cup chunky unsalted peanut butter

4 ounces bittersweet chocolate, coarsely chopped

Decorative sprinkles

In a mixing bowl, cream together the creamy peanut butter and sugar until lightened. Add the egg, vanilla, and cream and mix well.

In another mixing bowl, combine the flour, salt, and baking powder. Add to the first mixture and mix well. Wrap in plastic wrap and refrigerate for 1 hour or overnight.

Preheat the oven to 325°F. Lightly butter 2 baking sheets.

On a lightly floured work surface, roll out the dough to 1/4 inch thick. Cut into 2-inch hearts with a heart-shaped cookie cutter. Place on the prepared baking sheets and bake for 8 to 10 minutes, until golden brown. Allow to cool on a wire rack. When cooled, place a spoonful (about 3/4 teaspoon) of the chunky peanut butter on half of the hearts and make a sandwich by topping with the remaining hearts. Place the sandwiches on a wire rack over a piece of parchment paper.

To melt the chocolate, make a double boiler by covering a simmering saucepan of water with a stainless steel mixing bowl. Place the chocolate in the bowl and stir for approximately 10 minutes, until melted. Try not to let any of the steam or moisture from the pan get into the chocolate as it will make it stiff instead of creamy.

Using a pastry brush, brush a layer of chocolate on the top of each cookie sandwich. While the chocolate is still soft, sprinkle with decorative sprinkles. *Makes 2 dozen cookies*

Heart Pretzels

1 envelope active dry yeast

1 cup warm water

2 tablespoons extra virgin olive oil

1/2 teaspoon salt

3-1/4 cups unbleached all-purpose flour

2 tablespoons baking soda

2 tablespoons coarse salt

Dissolve the yeast in the water. Add the oil, salt, and 1-1/2 cups of the flour. Stir together until thoroughly combined. Add the remaining 1-3/4 cups flour and stir until the mixture begins to form a ball. Transfer to a lightly floured work surface and knead the dough until smooth, about 10 minutes. Cover the dough and let rest in a warm, draft-free place for 1 hour.

Divide the dough into 12 equal pieces and roll them into 1/2-inch-thick ropes. Shape each rope into a heart. Set aside to rest on a floured work surface for 30 minutes.

Preheat the oven to 475°F. Lightly oil a baking sheet.

In a wide, shallow saucepan, bring 4 cups of water to a boil and add the baking soda. With a spatula, transfer the pretzels to the boiling water and cook for 1 minute, until slightly firm. Remove with a skimmer, allowing most of the water to drip off, and place on the prepared baking sheet. Sprinkle with coarse salt and bake for 12 minutes, until golden brown. *Makes 12 pretzels*

Valentine Pear Cupcakes

THESE WHIMSICAL CUPCAKES ARE A LOVELY VALENTINE'S DAY PARTY TREAT. MAKE THE CUPCAKES
AND SUGARED FLOWERS AHEAD, AND FROST AND DECORATE JUST BEFORE SERVING.

1-1/2 cups safflower oil

3 cups peeled and diced pear

2 cups granulated sugar

1-1/2 teaspoons vanilla extract

2 eggs

3 cups unbleached all-purpose flour

1 teaspoon baking soda

1-1/2 teaspoons ground cinnamon

1/4 teaspoon salt

Preheat the oven to 325°F. Line the cups of a muffin pan with decorative muffin papers.

In a mixing bowl, combine the oil, pear, granulated sugar, vanilla, and eggs. Mix well. In another bowl, combine the flour, baking soda, cinnamon, and salt. Fold gently into the pear mixture and mix well. Spoon into the prepared muffin pans and bake for 20 to 25 minutes, until a toothpick inserted in the center comes out clean. Remove the muffins from the pan and cool on a wire rack.

SUGARED FLOWERS

2 egg whites, at room temperature

1/4 teaspoon water

An assortment of edible, organically grown flowers, such as chamomile, snapdragons, and Johnny-jump-ups

2 cups superfine sugar

1 cup heavy cream

2 tablespoons confectioners' sugar

Valentine message candies for garnish

To make the sugared flowers: Lightly beat the egg whites and water, until blended. Hold the flower petals with tweezers and brush with the egg white. Sprinkle with the sugar. Tap the tweezers gently to remove excess sugar. Place on a rack to dry.

Whip the cream to soft peaks. Whip in the confectioners' sugar until well combined and the cream is firm enough to spread. Top the cupcakes with the whipped cream and garnish with sugared flowers and valentine message candies. *Makes 12 cupcakes*

Red Hot Candy Applesauce

COOKING APPLES WITH THEIR SKINS ADDS COLOR TO THE APPLESAUCE.

USING A FOOD MILL REMOVES THE SKINS TO GIVE THE APPLESAUCE A SILKY FINISH.

6 Rome apples, seeded and cut into chunks

2/3 cup water

1/3 cup honey

1/2 teaspoon freshly ground cinnamon

3 tablespoons unsalted butter, melted (optional)

Red hot candies, for garnish

Place the apples, water, honey, and cinnamon in a saucepan. Cover and bring to a simmer over medium heat. Cook for 15 to 20 minutes, until tender. Pass the apple mixture through a food mill and stir in the butter. Allow to cool to room temperature and serve garnished with the candies. *Makes 2 cups applesauce*

Baked Apple Hearts

CHOOSE APPLES THAT HAVE A DEEP-SET STEM SO THAT WHEN CUT IN HALF, THEY RESEMBLE A HEART.

3 Red Delicious apples, cored and halved lengthwise
with stems left intact

2 tablespoons sugar

1/4 cup finely chopped, toasted walnuts

1/2 teaspoon ground cinnamon

3 tablespoons unsalted butter

Preheat the oven to 350°F. Butter a 9 by 13-inch baking dish.

Slice a very thin slice from the uncut side of each apple half in order to stabilize it. Place the apples skin-side down in the baking dish.

In a small mixing bowl, combine the sugar, walnuts, and cinnamon. Place 1/2 tablespoon of butter in each apple. Sprinkle each with 1 tablespoon of the walnut mixture. Bake for about 20 minutes, until soft. Serve at once. *Serves 6*

Metric Conversion Table

LIQUID WEIGHTS

U.S. Measurements	Metric Equivalents
1/4 teaspoon	1.23 ml
1/2 teaspoon	2.5 ml
3/4 teaspoon	3.7 ml
1 teaspoon	5 ml
1 dessert spoon	10 ml
1 tablespoon (3 teaspoons)	15 ml
2 tablespoons (1 ounce)	30 ml
1/4 cup	60 ml
1/3 cup	80 ml
1/2 cup	120 ml
2/3 cup	160 ml
3/4 cup	180 ml
1 cup (8 ounces)	240 ml
2 cups (1 pint)	480 ml
3 cups	720 ml
4 cups (1 quart)	1 liter
4 quarts (1 gallon)	3.8 liters

DRY WEIGHTS

U.S. Measurements	Metric Equivalents
1/4 ounce	7 grams
1/3 ounce	10 grams
1/2 ounce	14 grams
1 ounce	28 grams
1-1/2 ounces	42 grams
1-3/4 ounces	50 grams
2 ounces	57 grams
3-1/2 ounces	100 grams
4 ounces (1/4 pound)	114 grams
6 ounces	170 grams
8 ounces (1/2 pound)	227 grams
9 ounces	250 grams
16 ounces (1 pound)	464 grams

TEMPERATURES

Fahrenheit	Celsius (Centigrade)
32°F (water freezes)	0°C
200°F	95°C
212°F (water boils)	100°C
250°F	120°C
275°F	135°C
300°F (low oven)	150°C
325°F	160°C
350°F (moderate oven)	175°C
375°F	190°C
400°F (hot oven)	205°C
425°F	220°C
450°F (very hot oven)	230°C
475°F	245°C
500°F (extremely hot oven)	260°C

LENGTHS

U.S. Measurements	Metric Equivalents
1/8 inch	3 mm
1/4 inch	6 mm
3/8 inch	1 cm
1/2 inch	1.2 cm
3/4 inch	2 cm
1 inch	2.5 cm
1-1/4 inches	3.1 cm
1-1/2 inches	3.7 cm
2 inches	5 cm
3 inches	7.5 cm
4 inches	10 cm

APPROXIMATE EQUIVALENTS

1 kilo is slightly more than 2 pounds.

1 liter is slightly more than 1 quart.

1 centimeter is approximately 3/8 inch.

Recipes

Crafts

Resources

April Cornell
Stores nationwide
(802) 879-5100
www.aprilcornell.com
*Fabric-covered gift boxes,
holiday linens, and housewares*

Ben Franklin Crafts
Novato, CA
(415) 897-2231
*Heart-shaped wreath frames,
floral and craft supplies*

Crate & Barrel
Stores nationwide
Catalog (800) 323-5461
www.crateandbarrel.com
*Heart-shaped bakeware, cookie
cutters, holiday housewares,
candles, and table linens*

Ideal Stationers
Mill Valley, CA
(415) 383-2600
*Craft and office supplies, lucite
magnet frames, and ink-jet
transfer papers*

Jo-Ann Fabrics & Crafts
Stores nationwide
(877) 465-6266
www.joann.com
Sewing, floral, and craft supplies

Office Depot
Stores nationwide
Catalog (888) 463-3768
www.officedepot.com
*Office supplies and ink-jet
transfer papers*

Pinestreet Paperie
Sausalito, CA
(415) 332-0650
*Ribbon, gift wrap and boxes,
rubber stamps, and decorative
papers*

Pottery Barn
Stores nationwide
Catalog (800) 922-5507
www.potterybarn.com
*Picture frames, holiday
housewares, candles, and
table linens*

Sur La Table
Stores nationwide
Catalog (800) 243-0852
www.surlatable.com
*Heart-shaped bakeware and
cookie cutters*

Viking Homechef
Stores in California
www.homechef.com
*Heart-shaped bakeware and
cookie cutters*

Williams-Sonoma
Stores nationwide
Catalog (800) 541-2233
www.williams-sonoma.com
*Heart-shaped bakeware and
cookie cutters*

Index